Also, by Anthony B. Bonapart

Love of God and His Teaching

A Study of What Leads Children to Become Adults

Who Love God and Follow His Teachings

Dreams in Print

ANTHONY B. BONAPART

To order additional copies of this book, contact:
Bookwhip
1-855-339-3589
www.bookwhip.com

DREAMS IN PRINT

When I was a younger man, my work required me to travel to distant locations around the world. I would often rest from my toil by taking afternoon naps. Later, I would go to bed early and wake up at the break of the day. During my slumber, I would dream about things that at the time seemed to have nothing to do with my life. I would jump up from my afternoon nap or from bed at 3:00 a.m. to write down the vision. I felt the vision was waiting on the next electrical brain wave to pass by so it could attach itself to be transported to unknown regions and forgotten. Therefore, I rushed to write down what I had seen. Where the visions came from, I do not know. Why they came, I do not know, nor do I know where they went. But I have always felt that they must serve some purpose.

Anthony B. Bonapart

PREFACE

I started writing down thoughts and images that paraded through my mind in the early 1990s. This book is comprised of eleven short stories derived from that period of my life. This book guides the reader across a range of human emotions under six headings: Love, Reap, Racism, Morality, Self-Esteem, and Faith.

The stories delve into issues that greatly affect our society today. The world has changed so much since my younger years. Many things relating to technology, social institutions, and mankind's head-on collision with the environment are considered. As I started writing this book, I realized the world has become better at some aspects of life and much worse with others. We still believe that love conquers all while our relationships with our neighbors and the environment continue to deteriorate.

This book takes the reader to a world filled with love, pain, struggle, hope, and faith. A spiritual journey that reveals illusive forces, that shape our daily lives. The reader is forced to wonder about the meaning of life. Are we the captains of our ship sailing through life or part of a universe created by divine power and might?

CONTENTS

LOVE

A son learned that love is timeless when he embraced the hand of his long-lost father. He discovered the devotion his father had to his mother and her newborn child could not be defeated by death or the passing of time.

Two lovers separated by a vast ocean. The beautiful maiden waited patiently for the sea to return her lover. The voyager fought against the sea to reach the one he loved. When all hope was lost, the power of love prevailed.

REAP

Humankind has the technology to completely change the environment in which we live. When the Jawana people used their knowledge to destroy the environment and hunt animal species to near extinction, nature fought back.

"For whatsoever a man soweth, that shall he also reap." Galatians 6:7 (KJV)

RACISM

This story delved into deep seated beliefs that one race is master to all others. This belief has existed throughout human history. The story seeks to discredit the ideology of one race superior to another by drawing attention to a reflex that all people have in common.

MORALITY

In Genesis 3:5 (KJV), the Serpent said unto the woman, "For God doth know that in the day ye eat thereof, then your eyes shall be opened, and ye shall be as gods, *knowing good and evil*." This story reveals how wrong the serpent was, as humankind continues to struggle with what acts committed by people are deemed right and which acts are wrong.

The citizens of Amadea foolishly allow an eloquent speaker into their hearts and minds.

This story forces the reader to think before embracing an impassioned speaker who promises to turn their nation into a utopian society.

"He who hates, disguises it with his lips, And lays up deceit within himself."

Proverbs 26:24 (NKJV)

SELF ESTEEM

This story takes an amusing look at low self-esteem. An islander takes a vacation in the big city. He goes into a tavern where he meets a local resident. Within seconds the islander feels something is very wrong with his new acquaintance.

FAITH

This inspiring story shows the reader that with faith, all hope is not lost. The path of those who have faith can be changed from a bitter end to a new morning filled with hope.

This is a remarkable story about a man of faith who witnessed something in a nursery and dismissed it. Doubt convinced him to reject what his eyes had seen, and his heart embraced. The story asked readers to have faith in their intuition, even when the feelings do not make sense.

An old man who is ostracized by the community for his odd behavior is befriended by a young islander. Although the old man has only muttered unintelligible words for ten years, he talks intelligently to the lad. The young man's faith is rewarded with words of wisdom.

The African American community has been plagued by youth violence. Although many national and community leaders have addressed the issue, the violence persists. The foundation of the African American community was built on scripture. Thorns helps the reader apply a biblical perspective to this difficult issue.

Love

THE VOW

---

*E*rrol, leading his band across the desert, daydreams of his arrival home, and the festive reception his charming mother will formally decree for his return. He reflects on how she raised him to become the leader of his people. But the mental images are suddenly erased by a loud cry from his men. He is beckoned to the front of the caravan where he finds a human skeleton lying in the barren earth grasping a pouch in its right hand.

Errol clutched the fragile hand of the skeleton, dislodged the pouch, and immediately the remains wither into dust. Within the pouch, there is a roll of parchment, which has remained undamaged.

Errol unfolds the scroll and begins to read:

"My precious Sinem, I appeal to the Divine Creator to impel a person of virtue to this epistle that it may be delivered to you. I trod through all of Anatolia for a word of you and at last found that you dwell in the Tarsus valley. My spirit is drained; my trek to find you has ended here in this desolate place. Deprived of nourishment, I expend my final breath recording these words to you. I beg you to forgive me for joining a foolish quest. Still, the war is won, and our people are secure once again. Despite our victory, I am the sole survivor of my legion and weak from battle."

"My flower, the absence of your fragrance has weakened my heart." In Gadarenas I came upon a holy man. I asked, "What is the meaning of love?"

And he replied, "For you Anan, love is Sinem your comely wife, who unknown to you, bore you a son." Overflowing with joy, I asked the Holy Man to pray that I may hold my son's hand before I return to dust. He vowed that it would be so.

The prophecy filled my heart with joy. Therefore, I set out across the barren plains without companions. I am lost in the vast sea of sand and breathe my last breath with the vision of you engraved in my heart.

At which point, the words ended. Errol folded the scroll and placed it in his garment. Then he removed a locket from his satchel and gazed at the likeness of his beautiful mother, Sinem.

PASSION AND THE SEA

$\mathcal{E}$lias the voyager lost his ship to an uncharted reef. He has waited many months on the isle of Cyprus for a vessel to bear him home. He finally gained passage on a Portuguese frigate, but fate delivered the vessel into the path of a powerful tempest. The violent encounter thrashed the craft and immediately it sank into the Sea.

Elias reasoned that he and the crew had minutes before the vessel plunged into the depths. Feeling a sense of dread, he sat on the deck, pondering his fate with that of his beloved Tirsa. All his desire and dreams descended with this ship; for that reason, Elias thought back to the final dispatch he sent to Tirsa followed by her passionate reply:

"My Beloved Tirsa,

Today I stood on the seashore gazing out over the blue frontier that divides us. I consoled myself by saying this torment that inflicts my soul will shortly pass. The sailors of antiquity held that men of my character cannot hunger for a thing they have seen or touched; our only desire lies in discovering that which has never been uncloaked.

I held an audience with the wise men of the island. They asked me to show them a portrait of you. I asked, "How can a man find peace with such a maiden in his heart?" They answered, "Only a fool would give up a maiden such as you. For a maiden of such splendor exists only in the minds of men."

My love, I cannot express with words how I long for your touch. I stand nude in the sun to find relief from my grief and fight with the spirit that seeks to prod you from my heart. I fear that if we do not join soon, this body will cease to exist.

It is written that a man has no master on earth. I say nay, for I am a man of the world – "My Master is you."

"My Dearest Elias,

Daily, I walk up the mount to look at docking vessels hoping that one is ferrying the source of the flame within my heart."

I swim in the Sea for she is the one I rival for your affection. I ask her, "Why have you taken my love from me?" And she answers, "I have only taken the body of Elias for his spirit belongs to you. I have bestowed pearls and diamonds upon him, yet I am unable to sever you from his heart. Even now he ventures here to be in your arms, therefore, take him, as I've grown weary of the chase."

My sweet, how I pray that these words are true, with tears flowing from my eyes, I ask the village seer if we will ever be united again? She answers yes, "For where there is love, even death cannot tear asunder." I have waited for you these many months; I will wait for eons if you desire. And if death should take me before we join, my soul shall not pass if not with yours. The old ones teach us that if a woman possesses the spirit of love, then the man who placed it there cannot live life without first satisfying her craving for passion.

Suddenly, Elias is shaken from his dream by the stormy waters dashing against his body. The ship started to break up. He was cast down from the ship into the violent sea quickly sinking into the abyss. He was a powerful swimmer, but to the sea, he is but a ripple. With his endurance fleeting he fought to reach the surface. But alas, only his right hand pierced the surface.

In the ensuing months Tirsa received word of the ship's demise along with its entire crew. She kneeled alone at the top of the mount gazing upon the port with dagger drawn. Clasping the blade with both hands, she raised it above her head. She drove the weapon downward at her midsection, but a mighty hand stayed the blade's lethal thrust. She looked up and there stood, Elias.

Reap

THE LEGEND
OF THE CREATURE

$\mathcal{M}$y name is Aymil, the Patriarch of my village. The rainy season came upon my territory. We celebrated the return of the yearly rain by talking to our children about the earth. We explained the many

blessings that come from our crops, even blessings that come from respecting the animals that share our land. I decided to spend this day talking to my daughter Ashaki, who was seven years old.

We sat by the window gazing out at the stormy heavens while discussing the stars, flowers, and frogs. Before long, a distressing look came upon her face. I asked, "Ashaki, why the somber spirit?"

She said in a soft voice, "Father many of my playmates speaks of a ghastly thing called a monster, and it frightens me. What does this creature look like? Why does it exist to bring harm to others?"

I carefully thought about a way to explain this subject to her. I held my daughter closely, saying, "I will tell you a story that describes this beast in its true form so that you and people with moral strength will not follow its path of destruction."

There was a nation like ours that existed in a faraway land that flourished for a thousand years. The inhabitants were called the Jawana people. No nation could equal their cunning for they were master hunters and seafarers. They cherished the land using their tools and physical prowess to enjoy the rich harvest the land supplied.

As generations passed, the people abandoned the teachings of their ancestors. They wanted more from the land and began to plunder the earth to sustain their cravings. Then they cut down every standing tree within the realm while hunting the animals to near extinction.

Although their storage bins and cupboards were gorged with sustenance, they ventured into the sea with all manner of weapons to slay the majestic sea creatures. Later, they fashioned new hunting instruments and scaled the mountains to hunt those animals that fled. At night, people could hear the forest cry out in pain. Shortly, the forests stopped providing food and medicine for the people.

At which point my daughter asked me, " What became of the Jawana people?"

I hesitated to tell her, and then I said, "When the land could no longer sustain their carnage, they made a perilous trek across land to another territory. And like avenging angels the starved animals vanquished many along the trail. Even the birds of prey swooped down upon them and took many of the little ones away. Like a foul wind, death and pestilence followed them along the trail. Nevertheless, a small number made it to the new land and never repeated the past."

Then my daughter asked, "Where are those that survived because she was fearful of them?"

I answered in a solemn voice, "Do not fear them since you and I must right the vile deeds they wrought on the earth. Look yonder, they rest in the burial ground of your ancestors."

Racism

BLINK

My name is Komal. In the age of conquest for my nation, I grew to become the interpreter of the law and the overseer of this sacred scroll. My nation embodied three tribes that lived in serenity and good will for centuries until an Outsider appeared from the sky, causing the people to reveal a vile belief that had lain dormant within their souls.

On the day that the Outlander arrived, there was a deafening eruption in the great forest, and many of my people dashed to the woodland to see what caused the explosion. When they arrived, there emerged out of the smoke, a life that was alien to us. The Outlander's build was in like manner to ours, but the Outlander wore a protective covering about his head, adorned with a greenish outfit that sheltered his body from prying eyes.

Immediately, the people began to worship the Outlander as a god, and they proclaimed, "This is the one our ancestors said would come from the sky." Shortly thereafter, the Outlander was ushered into our place of worship to meet the rulers of our three tribes to resolve a dispute rooted in the times of our Forefathers.

The Outlander was asked to stand on a pillar in the center of the grand meeting place. Omri, ruler of the Yahona tribe came forth and said, "Our Forefathers instructed us to prepare for your arrival." Then he faced the crowd with raised hands and declared; "The exalted one has come to solve the great mystery" and turned to the Outlander, shouting;

"Tell us, which of the three tribes is the Supreme Race?"

Then Arik, ruler of the Hawazy tribe and Ajlan ruler of the Wilusa ordered their warriors together with their people to fill the great hall. The rulers were convinced the answer to the great mystery would finally be settled. I, Komal, appealed to the rulers to stop this madness and send the people home, but the people shoved me aside, and rushed to hear the Outlander speak.

The Outlander stared at the multitude and suddenly began to speak, saying, "I have chosen which of you is worthy to be called the Supreme Race." The crowd became excited and many came forward to hear.

Thoughtfully, the Outlander continued; "But before I reveal my choice, I must inquire about a trait common among all of you. As I look upon the multitude, I became aware of skin that close and open over your eyes. Therefore, one cannot be considered the Supreme Race if any one race shares similar attributes with other humans and even with beasts of burden. A Supreme Race must be solely distinct from all others to merit this recognition."

The three rulers became irritated, And Omri announced, "I will bring before you my strongest warrior, and he will control this oddity called Blinking. He will prove that my people are the Supreme Race." Likewise, Arik, and Ajlan presented their bravest warrior.

The three warriors stood in front of the Outlander for ten hours until it became exceedingly hot. The perspiration poured down their face. One by one they began to blink.

At that point, the Outlander declared, "I must go away," and the crowd yelled, "When will you return?"

And the Outlander replied, "I will return when one of your tribes rises above the need to blink."

Then we heard a whirling sound come from the sky. The Outlander walked outside. Heavy twine came down from the sky. The Outlander grabbed it and was pulled into the heavens.

The rulers were not content with the judgment made by the Outlander, resulting in a great battle between the three tribes.

The conflict was settled which allowed me to set down these words for history to judge. Let it be known that my people mastered the need to blink. All are now one with the Supreme Being. I declare this because I am the last of my nation, and as I record these words, I blink my last; take my last gasp, as I join them in death.

Morality

RIGHT AND WRONG

*M*y name is Binoba. When I grew to attain the age of twenty, I resolved to become a member of a religious order. I made this resolution because I felt as an ordained teacher; I could quiet the raging debate over what act is inherently wrong and what deed is considered right.

To prepare myself for this new life, I embarked on a pilgrimage around the world to discover what acts humanity deems just and unjust.

I set sail for Arabia. Upon arrival, I disembarked, and then walked to a nearby village. Upon entering the village, I beheld the people assembled in the square. A pauper was being judged for pilfering food to feed his family. The people shouted, "Condemn him to prison for that is the place where thieves should pay for their crimes."

Before long I asked an onlooker, "Do you feel that stealing is wrong?" And he answered, "Yes, for I am a merchant. If every citizen refused to pay for my goods, then I would become destitute like this vagabond." I considered the merchant's rationale and concluded that it was sound, still, man's strongest instinct is to survive. Was this person committing a crime or using the instinct instilled in him at birth?

Shortly, I continued my walkabout and came upon a great nation that was at war with another. I met two men on a dirt road discussing a murder that recently occurred. I said, "Tell me friends, is murder right or wrong?"

They stopped their prattle, looked upon me, then one of them responded, "You are a foolish one indeed, because murder is not allowed in any civilized nation."

Then I replied, "But your nation is at war with another, and many will die in battle."

And the one said, "We fight for freedom from our oppressors;" Then I asked, "Why did the person you speak of commit murder?" He answered, "The murderer is a slave who killed his master."

At that point we parted. I journeyed to the seacoast and boarded a ship bound for Africa. While aboard ship I met a charming maiden, who seemed troubled. I asked, "Fair maiden what country do you travel to?"

She said, "I do not know where this voyage will take me. I was ordered aboard this ship by the village elders."

I asked, "What crime did you commit?"

She replied, "I was exiled because of a night of passion with a married man who is wealthy and influential. Some will call my weakness a transgression, some will not. You see, I love him, and dreamed that somehow, we could be wedded. But rather than risk a scandal, the elders put me aboard this ship and told me never to return."

I looked at the maiden as tears flowed from her eyes and raised my head shouting; "How can a man determine right from wrong in a world such as this?"

I left the ship upon arrival at the coast of Africa. I walked to the highlands where I met a man cultivating his field. My journey left me close to starvation, So, I asked the farmer for water and bread.

But he rebuked me shouting, "Go from this place pauper, there is no food here for your kind."

Then I noticed bread on the window ledge of his house. I grabbed the bread and tried to flee, but he seized me from behind.

We scuffled for the loaf, but I thrust him aside and ran with him in pursuit. During the chase, my pursuer fell shattering his head against a rock. The blow was fatal. Later warriors from the village captured me, imprisoning me here. Now, I am recording my saga on the wall of my cell for posterity.

If you are reading this confession, then you must also be a prisoner; therefore, I say these parting words to you. "My name is Binoba. Although I slowly perish in this wicked land for what they call transgressions against the people, realize that I am guiltless, since I was only doing what was right."

THE NEW BEGINNING

$\mathcal{A}$rianna was the newly appointed overseer of the Constitution of an independent nation of immense wealth and power Amadea. Its long-standing position on freedom has earned its statesmen worldwide acclaim. So, being named overseer of the Constitution at the age of 90 was a great honor for Arianna, a position that many Amadeans hope to achieve because to be considered, you must have spent your life upholding and defending the nation's sovereignty.

The Constitution is stored in the beautiful Sentinel building and placed where the people could read about the founding of the nation inscribed so long ago. Arianna stood before the book greeting the people and coaxing them to read the hallowed words.

Arianna's favorite duty was to entertain children, who Amadeans call, "The future." The children would come in groups to view the book and ask questions. One day a group of twenty 10-year old children arrived all dressed in their bright blue & white school colors. Their eyes gleamed with excitement as they read the opening statements. But one of the little girls who had read passages from the Constitution, suddenly stood silent as if in deep thought.

Arianna saw the child's demeanor and asked, "Do you have questions about the Constitution?"

And the children said, "This is Chenda, she always asks questions." Then, all the children stopped and listened.

Chenda looked at Arianna and said, "I once read about a country that lost its freedom. The people suffered greatly at the hands of tyrants. Has our nation ever suffered so?"

Arianna carefully thought about her reply to Chenda. The children were standing and staring at Arianna. She told them to sit down facing the Constitution.

Arianna said, "Children, the history of our nation is ripe with controversy. Our forefathers made a lot of mistakes building this great nation. Their freedom was constantly threatened by nations along its borders and each time the enemy was defeated. The exploits of our fighting men and women grew and became legendary around the world; thus, no nation would dare threaten our nation's sovereignty. Over time, our forefathers became boastful and failed to see the threat growing from within." They failed to recognize an articulate speaker's true intentions.

Then Chenda said, "But now we are taught to be mindful of people who proclaim the truth while hiding bad intentions."

Arianna replied, "Yes, Chenda. Now let me tell you why Amadean children are taught to beware of people who work to uplift the nation while hiding their sinister ulterior motive.

And Arianna said, "Long ago, there was a man named Abaddon who rose to prominence in Amadea. He was a poor man of little consequence, but blessed with the ability to deliver eloquent speeches. He became engrossed in the politics of the time and used his charisma to gain influential positions in the ruling party."

He often spoke of transforming Amadea into a utopian society where everyone benefited from Amadea's economic prosperity. His beliefs attracted certain wealthy members of the society and religious leaders who saw an opportunity to use Abaddon to fulfill their quest for power.

Abaddon knew how to move the people. So, the rich and powerful conspired to use their money to fund his rise to power. Religious leaders attracted by his charisma used their platform to boost his image and message. The ministers even gathered millions of followers to witness Abaddon receive the prestigious Book of Prayers. As time passed, the people began to worship Abaddon. In response, he traveled to distant parts of the nation to deliver impassioned speeches. Eventually, Amadeans elected Abaddon to lead the nation. He proclaimed the day of his inauguration "A New Beginning."

He ordered the people to gather in a large field to take part in a grand parade to celebrate his "New Beginning." He decreed that his wealthy supporters and religious leaders would lead the procession. The judges were told to remove the Constitution from the Sentinel building with all the accompanying books. They were told to raise the Constitution as they marched to show the people that Abaddon believed in freedom.

He directed the men and women of law to bring the nation's great books of justice. They were ordered to hold the books high to represent Abaddon's respect for truth and honesty. He summoned the esteemed historians and asked them to bring the nation's history books. He ordered the heads of all government agencies to join the parade and bring the statues that created their institution. And he ordered Uriah, Commander of the Army and all the military chiefs to march in the rear of the procession. A marching band was assembled to play patriotic music.

On that fateful day, Abaddon stood in front of the great procession. The judges stood proudly in formation holding the Constitution and all the great books in which our forefathers recorded the nation's history as the people gathered to watch the parade.

The procession was ordered to face east. The wealthy that funded Abaddon's rise to power was first. The ministers stood proudly with the wealthy smiling and waving at the people.

The children who represented the future stood in formation behind them. The judges holding the Constitution and accompanying books stood behind the future. The historians proudly carried the books containing the names of the great men and women who founded the nation and fought for freedom. The leaders of every agency representing the nation's system of government stood behind the historians proudly carrying the statues that created their institution.

When the parade was about to start, a dense bank of fog rolled in from the east where the procession was heading. Nevertheless, Abaddon ordered the band to strike up the patriotic music. The people yelled, "Abaddon is great," as the procession marched east toward the fog.

No one knew the destination of the procession. The rich citizens and ministers leading the procession followed the directions of Abaddon. The band played patriotic music as they marched, and Abaddon directed the procession using a Bull Horn.

The procession streamed into the fog with people cheering and Abaddon telling the lead group to press forward for the future of Amadea. Then, shortly after entering the fog, the lead group of the procession disappeared. Among the children who marched behind the lead group was a 12-year-old boy named Boman. He was blind and sensed something unexpected ahead and he yelled, "STOP."

The fog was thick, making it impossible for the people to see. The members of the procession became frightened. Boman, yelled out to Abaddon, "Sir, why are you not leading us into the future?"

Abaddon replied out of the mist, "I will lead you to a new future one of my designs."

Boman said, "Then why not carry our Constitution with you?" Abaddon replied, "I will write a new Constitution conceived from my mind."

Then Bowman said, "A new Constitution must be based on our nation's history which cannot be changed."

Abaddon laughed and said, "I will re-write the nation's past with people who look and act as I see fit. A history that will glorify me as the nation's founder,"

Then, Shabaka a distinguished professor of science, born with an affliction to his right arm, stepped forth and asked, "But what about people who look like me?"

Abaddon replied, "The future for people like you lie ahead, that is why you must keep marching."

Abaddon became angry because the Constitution was being carried behind the future who held up the procession, and he ordered the military leaders to call up their fighting men and women to push the procession forward.

But Uriah refused, saying, "The Constitution forbids the military from forcing its will upon the people."

Then the fog began to dissipate, and the people saw Abaddon standing along the edge of a cliff. Abaddon became frightened as the people moved toward him and he ran not aware of his position and tumbled over the cliff. He fell screaming into the abyss.

And the people looked down and could see no bottom. The people yelled out, "Where are the wealthy and the ministers?" Then, the people cried in sorrow as they realized that Abaddon tried to lead the whole nation over a Cliff. The people returned the Constitution to its place of honor in the Sentinel building.

Self Esteem

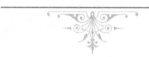

THE NOBODY
CONVERSATION

The summer months were extremely hot on my island; so, I decided to take a vacation in the big city to escape the sweltering heat. The city was the playground for many influential people: actors who we call stars to associate them with celestial bodies. There are artists, athletes, businessmen and women, journalists, and the world's most eccentric chefs.

I secured a modest hotel room and passed the day by taking daily walks throughout the city. One day, I decided to stroll down to the local tavern situated along the shore to partake of the complimentary buffet.

While I sat quietly dining a curious man approached me.

He stared at me, smiled, and said, "I have admired your paintings for years, aren't you one of our local artists?"

I replied, "Thank you for your kind words, but you are confused." I extended my hand in friendship and said, "My name is Efrem."

Surprisingly, he withdrew his hand and stepping back said, "I apologize for the interruption, however, since you are nobody, no disrespect intended, I will retire from this conversation and leave you in peace."

"A nobody!" I exclaimed; then I regained my composure, said "Excuse me, what is the definition of nobody?"

Well, said the gentleman, "I do not want to demean you in any way. Nonetheless, nobody is a person of no influence or worth, and you fit the description." I have memorized the definition and spent my professional career studying outcomes of people's lives, so I am aware of what nobody is.

I asked, "What is your profession?"

He declared with vigor. "I am a renowned compost collector."

He then turned silently to receive some people who were adorned in the finest attire, with the most precious stones one could acquire. I watched in bewilderment as the party sat at a table and exchanged pleasantries. He collected their litter and deposited it in his receptacle. He joyfully looked at the refuse he had collected.

Later, as the party was leaving the tavern, the gentleman turned to face me. He gazed at the people's trash he collected and then announced, "See, see, now these people are somebody."

Perplexed, I stared at them as they left the tavern immersed in self-consumption. I suspected that there must be inner turmoil for people who measure their worth by the people they consort with. They further compensate for feelings of inferiority by convincing themselves, they are superior to others. Nevertheless, the gentleman confirmed what I always suspected: if one desires to be important, but life has not propelled them to that status, one does not have to spend years studying the customs and habits of the rich and famous. To learn their habits and master their traits, you must simply become a connoisseur of the garbage they cast aside.

Faith

CRESTFALLEN

In the village of Izmir, it was the time of year to honor the harvest by celebrating with a great feast. Chefs would prepare glorious meals for all the people, a banquet with the most popular dishes found in the culture. But this day, one of the villagers named Tasha secretly strolled away to the nearby cliff's edge to ponder her fate.

Tasha was a young girl of sixteen years who felt exhausted from the burdens of life. She gazed at the peaceful sea, tearfully deciding that the calm waters would be her final resting place. She prayed as she prepared to jump, but hesitated because her mind was replaying all the mistakes she had made. She thought about how hard she tried to make everything right, but no matter what she did or who aided her, things got worse.

She took one last gasp of air, and then leaped, but alas she did not jump out far enough from the cliff's edge, landing screaming on the ridge below. Suddenly, a man called out to her, "Young lady are you alright?" Then a strong hand pulled her up from the crest as she fainted.

The man wrapped a warm coat around her, quickly took her to his home. Later she awoke. Looking around her savior's residence, she asked, "Where is this place?"

The man said, "You are in a house of worship. I am a priest who fortunately pulled you from the crest."

Then Tasha with tears in her eyes said, "How is it that I end up with a Holy Man in whom I have never confided, in a house of worship, which I have never visited."

The priest said, "Do you not remember your last words before you jumped?"

Tasha replied, "I do not recall my last words."

Then the priest said, "I saw you standing on the cliff's edge and immediately started towards you. However, I could not reach you in time, but the Divine One can achieve what man cannot because before you jumped, you cried out "God help me".

NEWBORNS

Takur, elder statesman of his village lay at death's door. The shadow of the reaper descended upon his face beckoning him to join his ancestors in the great unknown. Envisioning his impending demise, Takur summoned his disciples to gather before him.

He spoke, "Children, in my dreams I beheld the angel of death preparing my carriage, therefore, draw near and listen as I reveal a vision of which I have never spoken.

When I was a young man, there came a glorious day when twelve maidens, one by one bore a babe within the same hour. The occasion created a festive mood throughout the valley. Even the sun illuminated the multitude with its radiance. As I strolled to the home of the midwife to behold the beautiful infants, my heart was inspired by this celebration of life. Arriving at the cottage, I glanced through the entrance at the little ones and immediately noticed a glimmer of light that surrounded the babies. This mystic appearance astonished me. I assumed the excitement had overwhelmed me and caused the delusion. Furthermore, the cottage was bustling with people who carried on joyfully with no perception of the gentle gleam of light.

I summoned the midwife and asked, "Do you notice anything peculiar about these toddlers?" She replied, "No, they are just babies," and continued her chores. I decided to withdraw from the cottage; however I became motionless as my eyes were drawn into the light.

I beheld the babies smiling as they looked up at the heavens. I saw a mentor in the form of a cloud and the infants engrossed in a tutorial. The mentor possessed great wisdom, passing on the knowledge of the world to the infants. I heard, the cloud speak, saying: "Pay homage to the one who bathed you in the light of the sun, for the breath of life that flows within you is the Revered One's essence. Today is your alpha; exalt your mother and father until your life's omega. Beware, even now, minions of evil are preparing temptations for you."

Suddenly, I was aroused from my daydream by a soft shake. I looked and there stood a petite, devout woman whom I had never seen. She said to me: "The newborns look as if they are talking to angels, don't they?" Then she slowly walked away.

I share this story with you so that you do not abandon your faith as easily as I. My heart dismissed what my eyes witnessed. A foul spirit entered my mind and convinced me to reject the vision. Thus, I failed to announce the good news of the coming joy these babies would help usher into the world. I was wrong.

What became of the children you ask? "They grew, and then left the village to pursue their calling. However, fate chose them to become emissaries of peace and love. Their legacy spreads even as we speak. Only one of the twelve succumbed to evil."

THE CENTENARIAN

There is a grand tradition on my island called the Day of Prosperity. On this day we walk into the homes of those who have persevered to live a hundred years. We celebrate their life with dancing followed by a great feast. There was one centenarian whose name was Jairus. He had not engaged in conversation with his fellow neighbors for over 10 years. When you approached him to determine his soundness of mind, he only uttered "The answer is not out of you;" Only these few words did he speak for over a decade.

People shunned him because of his curious behavior. But on this festive night, I decided to visit him and sit quietly by his side. He sat in front of his bungalow beneath a tall woody plant staring at the moon. I sat humbly next to him. After an hour had gone by, I decided to depart, leaving him engrossed in his meditations.

As I attempted to quietly leave, he grabbed my hand. He asked, "What is your name child?

I replied, "My name is Hatice."

He said, "Hatice you believe me to be mad, do you not?"

I answered, "Some say that you are, regardless, I have come to find out for myself. The words you speak have no meaning to us; therefore, it is natural that some will consider you crazed."

Then he said, "People will follow the guidance of those who have attained great wealth and influence in the society. Some will even reap praise upon them as they speak with energy, conviction, and vigor while saying nothing of substance. Yet, I speak little, say much, and deemed deranged."

Behold, humans continually seek answers to problems that directly affect them. They search the hills and valleys while never looking inward for the answer.

There was a time when gloom routed my spirit. I joined a caravan and searched 20 years seeking why life had crushed me so brutally. But one day as I sat on a mountainside, pondering the failure of clerics, intellects, and prudent men to adequately interpret my torment. I beheld an ant trying to pull back to its lair a portion of an apple that was elephantine in relation to its tiny build. I observed the ant struggle with this burden from midday till twilight. Suddenly the ant bit off a small section of the apple and meandered away. You see, we humans take on burdens that are too great to attain, just like the ant. But the ant surmised how to solve the problem by taking only what it could bear, discarding the rest of the world to divide.

THORNS

$\mathcal{I}$ am called Silas. A storm drove me to a remote village where I begged for food and shelter. I wandered the land unnoticed for many years. But when I entered this village, the people were gathered in the village square for prayer. One of the villagers named Nijah recognized me as I approached. Startled by my appearance, she yelled, "Silas, where have you been, and why are you living like a vagabond?" Nijah quickly summoned the village elders and told them that I was once a great physician. She then turned to me and said, Silas "Tell us what happened."

There I stood motionless, dressed in ragged clothing looking at the people. The crowd grew larger waiting for me to reply. Then I said, "Yes, I was once a physician engaged in a prosperous practice. But a fateful encounter persuaded me to forego my profession to pursue a more noble cause."

One of the villagers shouted sarcastically, "Why to leave a life of plenty to become a beggar?" (*Laughter*)

I replied, "The event that altered my life came to pass many years ago. After caring for a patient, I bid farewell and turned to board my carriage for home. A beautiful maiden approached me as I climbed aboard. She was smiling and full of life.

She said, "Sir, how could you ride on such a beautiful day. A walk revives the soul. At midday stroll could even change your outlook on life."

Her soothing voice convinced me to walk; so, I dismissed the coachman. The maiden smiled and continued down the road.

My village was situated near the river. Seeing that it was midday and sunny I decided to take the river path home. Shortly into my walk, I came upon a young man crawling out of a thorny bush towards the bank of the river. I turned him over and saw blood flowing from his midsection. Hastily, I ministered to his wounds, but he stopped me and begged me to listen.

In a somber voice, he said, "Your appearance is that of a learned man. Looking at me in this dire condition, you would not believe that I aspired to become an educated man. **It is written that seeds planted among thorns will fail to flourish**. I was raised in a village devoid of mercy and consumed by strife. We, the young men, preyed upon each other, killing without purpose or reason. As children, we would gather in the square to watch actors reenact killings and listen to songs that celebrated murder. I was convinced that I had to become ruthless to survive.

I joined a band of young rebels who robbed and killed for money. As time passed, the men and women of faith would invite me into their sanctuary and place me in the seat of kings. They would accept my money and call me great! Then, I would gather my gang and leave the sanctuary to wreck more havoc upon the community. We used our spoils to pay for lavish parties. During the revelry, we consumed all manner of drugs and plotted more criminal acts. We would go out into the streets and chase our enemies into their neighborhoods and homes. And we killed them with little regard to the terror we wrought upon the people.

But one day, my heart grew weary of the violence. I longed for a better life and found a way to escape. When the way was clear, I hastily left my village; but young men were seeking to avenge those I had harmed, and they set upon me as I traveled on the road. For days I wandered aimlessly and now the chill of death is upon me.

Perhaps, if I had someone like you to help me, I would have succeeded."

Then I said, "Son, I will help you. Hold my hand while I bind your wounds. He looked at me and said, "Sir, I have thorns stuck all over my body – I could not escape". Then he died.

As I held the young man and grieved over his death, a spirit entered my mind. I was led to a field of thorns where thousands of young men were killing each other. The spirit beckoned me to come closer to the fallen youth and revealed they were mirror images of each other. All were raised in a field of thorns that prevented the growth of their minds. They were not raised on scripture, and their roots were buried deep in the thorns. Thus, they killed the future of their people.

At that moment, I decided to dedicate my life to help replant the minds of young men. I left my profession and joined a sect of holy men dedicated to planting the minds of youth in good soil.

Then Silas turned to the people and said, "You called me a beggar! The sound of your prayers came to me through the storm, and the spirit led me to your doorstep. I am not a beggar but have come to replant the young men that you prayed for on earth seeded by the scriptures. Thereby, giving them the strength to leave the field of thorns and walk the good earth." A mother with her two teenage sons heard Silas speak and immediately realized he was a holy man. She walked up to Silas and knelt before him. Then Silas, Nijah, and all the elders bowed down and began to pray.

CPSIA information can be obtained
at www.ICGtesting.com
Printed in the USA
LVHW090435201120
672005LV00008B/584